WORSHIPPING GOD
ALPHABETICALLY

WORSHIPPING
GOD
ALPHABETICALLY

HOMER L. ISAAC, JR.

XULON PRESS

Xulon Press
2301 Lucien Way #415
Maitland, FL 32751
407.339.4217
www.xulonpress.com

Paperback ISBN-13: 978-1-6628-4504-8
Ebook ISBN-13: 978-1-6628-4689-2

Table of Contents

Introduction

This book is a compilation of twenty-six scripturally based, thought provoking poems. Each poem begins with the corresponding letter of the alphabet and the first letter of the scripture on which the poem is based. Most include an encouraging word or meditative thought, and related lyrics taken from an appropriate song, or adage. These poems are not written, intended to be, nor, should they be construed as scholarly works. They are written with the sole purpose of providing encouragement to you in your daily worship relationship with God. May you be blessed as you meditate and read each one.

A Scripture

But the hour cometh, and now is, when the true worshippers shall worship the Father in spirit and in truth: for the Father seeketh such to worship him (John 4:23).

A Word

"God would not be worthy of our worship if He could be understood by our wisdom".[1]

A Song

My faith looks up to Thee
Thou Lamb of Calvary
Savior divine!
Now hear me while I pray,
Take all my guilt away,
O let me from this day
Be wholly Thine![2]

Chapter One

And Be Not Conformed

And be not conformed to this world: but be ye transformed by the renewing of your mind, that ye may prove what is that good, and acceptable, and perfect, will of God (Romans 12:2).

And be not conformed to this world:
but be ye transformed
by the renewing of your mind,
a transformative renewal of a spiritual kind.
What the psychologist refers to as a
modification of behavior,
to the Christian, it's living a new life and trusting
the word of Our Lord and Savior.

The song writer/performer Curtis Mayfield
of late, penned these
words to which many of us can relate:

"Why don't you check out your mind
Been with you all the time
People thinking they been 'took'

Just finding out they overlooked
They never found the missing link
Forgot they had a mind to think"[3]

Our minds refuse to let go of the question
we asked God in prayer
(Who we thought hadn't answered yet, or didn't care).
But in fact, He'd answered so long ago,
that we almost forgot that He had responded
with a loving "no".

We continue to ask, "Who is my father?
or why he didn't want to be a bother,
or what kind of mother would give a baby away,
only to face the ensuing criticism, inuendo and hearsay?

Apparently, there are things God knows that
we don't need to know in order for us
to become spiritually mature and continue to grow.

The thoughtless action, mistake or temptation of an
adult, often negatively affects other innocent
lives significantly as result.
Some of those actions that have affected our lives carry
artificial guilt, heartache and pain, causing us to run in
place, but making no gain.

We need to renew our minds and trust that only God
knows what we need to know for our minds to be
transformed, yielded and still,

"That we may prove what is His good, acceptable, and perfect will."

Have Thine Own Way

Have thine own way, Lord!
Have thine own way!
Thou art the potter,
I am the clay.
Mold me and make me
after thy will,
while I am waiting,
yielded and still.[4]

Related Rhetorical Questions

- Do you see yourself in any part of this poem?
- Can you think of someone else to whom this poem resonates?
- Is this poem worth reading again?
- Do you agree with the statement: "The more I study the Word of God, the more I know that I need to study the Word of God more".

Personal Notes

_____

_____

_____

_____

_____

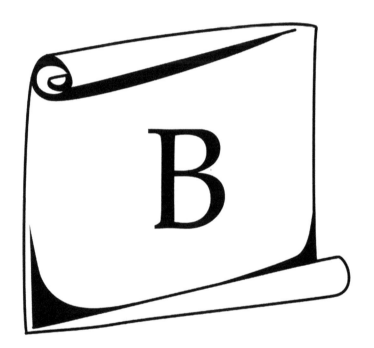

Chapter Two

Bless the Lord, O My Soul

Bless the LORD, O my soul: and all that is within me, bless his holy name (Psalms 103:1).

Bless the Lord, O my soul and all that is within me.
Bless? How could we even consider doing
anything less?

And *all* that is within me, from the top of my head to
the soles of my feet
I should be praising the Lord continuously,
without ever missing a beat.

For all God has done, is doing and is able to do, no
one has an excuse not to bless Him, including me;
including you.
And, if we are truly honest, there are many blessings
that have been bestowed on us, that we have taken for
granted without even making a fuss.

How many times have we fallen asleep without blessing
the Lord, too tired to get down on our knees and
bow our head?

Never pausing to think of the dangers seen and un-seen
that God has protected us from. Serious harm, injury,
or, we could have been dead.
What good will it do us if we set our alarm clock,
cell phone or other electronic device,
If we don't bless God for loving us enough to save us
through His only son, Jesus Christ.
The One who gave His life for my sins that I might be
forgiven for all of my transgressional mess,
By removing these transgressions (according to
Psalm 103:12) "as far as the east is from the west".
I will bless the Lord for He has created
the stars and every planet.
I will never take His love, grace or mercy
towards me for granted.

The mercy of the Lord," *is from everlasting to ever-
lasting upon them that fear Him and his righteousness
unto children's children" (Psalm 103:17).*

So, as I humbly bow in trepidation, I will bless
the Lord as my sacred obligation,
that the mercy of the Lord will pass down to
yet another future generation,

Related Rhetorical Questions

- Do you see yourself in any part of this poem?
- Can you think of someone else to whom this poem resonates?
- Is this poem worth reading again?
- Do you agree with the statement: "The more I study the Word of God, the more I know that I need to study the Word of God more".

Personal Notes

_____

_____

_____

_____

_____

_____

_____

Chapter Three

Create In Me a Clean Heart

Create in me a clean heart, O God; and renew a
right spirit within me (Psalm 51:10).

Create in me a clean heart. I need a fresh start. I confess
to you my sin and ask
You to renew a right spirit within.
I have not always done what You told me to do
and I have done some things
You told me not to do.
For my sins of omission and commission
I pray dear Lord for remission.
I used to pray by repetition, "Now I lay me down to
sleep, I pray the Lord my soul to keep."
But as I matured and life got 'deep', sometimes
I had to cry out, moan and even weep.
I have allowed my clean heart to become impure, by a
lust for greed, self-ambition and desires
that were immature.
People in positions in law enforcement and most
public officials take a vow, under oath,
while holding a Holy Bible.

In moments of weakness, however, those vows
that were taken with good intentions, are ignored
for self-survival.

Lord, in order for me to worship you in spirit and in
truth, I need you to give me a clean heart
so that I may serve you.
Help me to speak up for Your law, so true.
Even if it means going against political correctness
or "codes of silence" (red, white or blue).
Let me not be ashamed to stand up for your Holy Name,
nor fail to speak with intestinal fortitude.
But help me to speak Your Word with boldness,
unashamedly, yet with a Holy attitude.

Speak to my Heart

Speak to my heart, Holy Spirit
Give me the words that will bring new life
Words on the wings of a morning,
the dark night will fade away
If You speak to my heart now[5]

Related Rhetorical Questions

- Do you see yourself in any part of this poem?
- Can you think of someone else to whom this poem resonates?
- Is this poem worth reading again?
- Do you agree with the statement: "The more I study the Word of God, the more I know that I need to study the Word of God more".

Personal Notes

_____

_____

_____

_____

_____

_____

_____

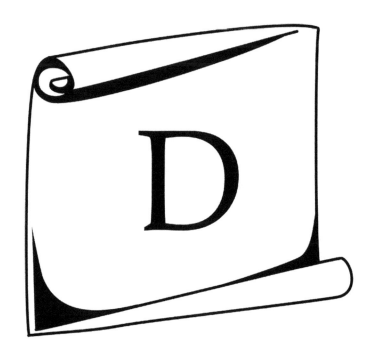

Chapter Four

Delight Thyself in the Lord

*Delight thyself also in the LORD: and he shall give
thee the desires of thine heart (Psalm 37:4).*

Delight thyself also in the Lord, let your will be
absorbed into His will from the start. Promise Him
that from His will, you won't ever depart.
He will then place you into a position to receive the
desires according to His will for you. These now
become the desires of your heart.

Your desire could be to have a beautiful fur coat
(or two, if you are greedy).
But His will might be for you to have only one. Giving
the other to the needy.

The desire you may have to retire, relax and have
an occasional cold beer,
might be interrupted by His will for you to work
as a nursing home volunteer.

It might be your will to have great finances and never
be in want or broke.
Whatever His will, His burden is light and He is right
beside you in your "yoke".

There will be times your heart may desire to stray from
God's commandments no matter how slight.
Be strong in the Lord and the power of His might.
Before you know it that temptation will fade from sight.
Don't be discouraged when it seems like the wicked
always get off, never paying "the bill", while the rest of
us are doing our best to live according to God's will.
I would rather live right and be ridiculed, but with my
Savior dwell, than to live according to the carnal desires
of my heart and spend eternity in hell.
The desires of my heart are not what they used to be, as
God spiritually and continuously matures me.
As I press on toward the mark of the high calling set for
me, I praise God for setting me free of selfish desires
that I no longer see.

"If the Son therefore shall make you free,
ye shall be free indeed." (John 8:36).

I'm Free

I'm free
Praise the Lord, I'm free
No more longer bound
No more chains holding me
Soul is resting
And it's just another blessing
Praise the Lord!
Hallelujah, I'm free[6]

Related Rhetorical Questions

• Do you see yourself in any part of this poem?
• Can you think of someone else to whom this poem resonates?
• Is this poem worth reading again?
• Do you agree with the statement: "The more I study the Word of God, the more I know that I need to study the Word of God more".

Personal Notes

_____

_____

_____

_____

_____

_____

_____

Chapter Five

Enter His Gates

Enter into his gates with thanksgiving, and into his
courts with praise be thankful unto him and bless
his name (Psalm 100:4).

Enter His gates with thanksgiving I learned as a child.
But at the time I didn't realize,
that was exactly what my mother was doing first
when she entered service, bowed her head and
closed her eyes.
I'm sure she thanked God for the end of another week
reached, and another opportunity
to hear the Word preached.
Entering His gates first giving "thanks", shows God
how important "thanks" is on our priority prayer list,
and where on that list it ranks.
By beginning service with an attitude of gratitude the
tone is set, for you to petition God for your
needs to be met.
It seems to me that over the years worshippers
have changed, and the priority of our prayer list
has been rearranged.

I wonder how much better we would be if we started
our worship services with prayers of thanks,
instead of thinking about the amount of money
God has put into our banks.
Now don't get me wrong, I too am guilty of "prayer
corruption" and I too fear for that voice of interruption.
The voice of One who helps us most, to do what's right,
yes, the Holy Ghost.
Entering His gates with thanksgiving is certainly the
first thing I must do as part, to make room for what
God wants to instill in my heart.
After all, if I come out of the temple the same way
I entered, maybe I need to enter the temple again, ...only
this time with a prayer of thanksgiving and for the
forgiveness of my sin.

House of the Lord

I was glad when they said unto me,
let us go into the house of the Lord.
There's no better place to be,
there's peace and liberty,
let us go into the house of the Lord.

A day in His house is better
than thousand days anywhere else.
I'd rather be a doorkeeper in my Father's house
than to have a palace all by myself.[7]

Related Rhetorical Questions

- Do you see yourself in any part of this poem?
- Can you think of someone else to whom this poem resonates?
- Is this poem worth reading again?
- Do you agree with the statement: "The more I study the Word of God, the more I know that I need to study the Word of God more".

Personal Notes

_____

_____

_____

_____

_____

_____

_____

Chapter Six

For All Have Sinned

For all have sinned and come short of
the glory of God (Romans 3:23).

For all have sinned and come short of His glory,
which should make for a very short story.
Except our gracious heavenly Father above, the world
so much did love
That He sent His only begotten son, to atone
for what we had done.
What a merciful God we serve, who would give us an
opportunity to believe in His Son and avoid the
wages of sin that we deserve.
Sin that is punishable by death, if we have not con-
fessed, believed and repented before we have taken
our last breath.
How many obituaries have we read, littered with words
of obsession, where there was no mention of confession
by the one now dead,
The deceased was the "nicest" person you ever
met. Never got upset. He had lots of friends and
a great reputation.

But not one of those friends took the time to lead him to
seek salvation and keep him from eternal damnation.
Was it you? Was it me? Did we waste an opportunity?
Oh Lord, please forgive me of my sins of omission
as well as my sins of commission.
I thank you for reminding me that I am the only
"church" some will ever see. Please give me the courage
I need for this mission, to help someone who is in a
fallen condition.

Lord, Lay Some Soul

*Lord lay some soul upon my heart and love that soul
through me. And may I bravely do my part to win that
soul for thee.*[8]

Related Rhetorical Questions

- Do you see yourself in any part of this poem?
- Can you think of someone else to whom this poem
  resonates?
- Is this poem worth reading again?
- Do you agree with the statement: "The more I study
  the Word of God, the more I know that I need to
  study the Word of God more".

Personal Notes

_____

_____

_____

_____

_____

_____

_____

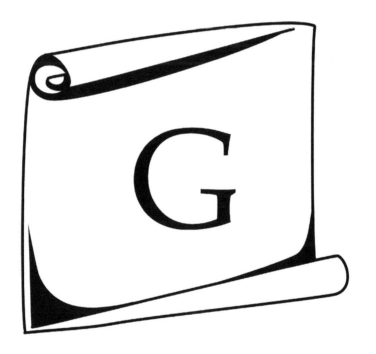

Chapter Seven

God Is Our Refuge and Strength

God is our refuge and strength, a very present
help in trouble (Psalms 46:1).

God is our refuge and strength, a very present help in
trouble. Since He is already here, there is no reason to
pray for Him to come, 'on the double'.
It doesn't matter if you are big, strong and brawny,
or meek, tiny and scrawny.
Sooner or later, you will need to call on God your
maker when you get into a situation that's
a real 'earth shaker'.
How often do we hear someone say, "I'm a grownup
man!" Thinking, anything that needs
to be done, 'he can'.
But there are dangers yet seen and unseen for which
we are not prepared to face, when we will need
to seek a refuge or a hiding place.
God is our refuge and strength, a very present help in
trouble, for anyone whether you have smoothed skin or
have a chin full of man-like stubble.

There is no shame to call upon His name.
Swallow your pride and let Him abide.
Come boldly before His throne of grace.
You don't have to hide your face.
Christ died for our sins and took our place,
don't continue to suffer disgrace.
Call out to the God of our salvation and receive
your vindication.
The Apostle Paul declared that when he was
made weak, he was made strong.
When God is your refuge and strength,
we can sing that 'same song'.
Stay on the battlefield and it won't be long before you
find out that in God's refuge you were safe all along.

On the Battlefield

I am on the battlefield for my Lord,
I'm on the battlefield for my Lord;
And I promised Him that I would serve Him till I die.
I am on the battlefield for my Lord.[9]

Related Rhetorical Questions

- Do you see yourself in any part of this poem?
- Can you think of someone else to whom this poem resonates?
- Is this poem worth reading again?
- Do you agree with the statement: "The more I study the Word of God, the more I know that I need to study the Word of God more".

Personal Notes

_____

_____

_____

_____

_____

_____

_____

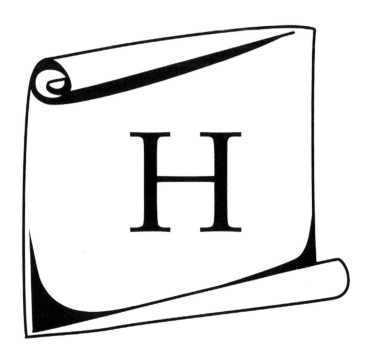

Chapter Eight

Hear O Israel

Hear, O Israel: The LORD our God is one LORD
(Deuteronomy 6:4)

Hear, O Israel: The Lord our God is one Lord,
in the Bible we are told.
So, how did we forget so quickly,
how did we become so cold?
How cheaply was our soul sold?

"In the beginning God...."
"In the beginning was the word, and the word
was with God, and the word was God."
"But seek ye first the kingdom of God..."
Before we became a "Nation under God",
there was God.
Before we made our motto, "In God we trust",
there was God.
Before we decided which one of the races created by
God would be inferior and which one would be
superior, there was God.

Before we erroneously accepted that the love of money
was *not* the root of evil, there was God.
Before we spinelessly abandoned our vows that we took
before God to preserve the Constitution, there was God.
Before we lost our moral compass and forgot our obli-
gation to speak up against a wrong with the vow we
took to protect and defend, there was God.
Before we lost our self-respect and accepted leaders
that constantly spew vile, vulgar and vindictive filth
from their mouths, there was God.
So, where is God now? God is where God always was/
is/shall be. It is my heart that moved away from God's
love and greatness.
I can publicly protest in order to draw attention
to a problem, or insist on enacting laws that
help to solve them.
I can retrain and re-organize in an attempt to humanize.
All to no avail if I don't remember still that...
The Lord our God is one Lord.

Great is Thy Faithfulness

Great is Thy faithfulness, O God my Father
There is no shadow of turning with Thee
Thou changest not, Thy compassions, they fail not
As Thou hast been Thou forever wilt be.[10]

Related Rhetorical Questions

- Do you see yourself in any part of this poem?
- Can you think of someone else to whom this poem resonates?
- Is this poem worth reading again?
- Do you agree with the statement: "The more I study the Word of God, the more I know that I need to study the Word of God more".

Personal Notes

_____

_____

_____

_____

_____

_____

_____

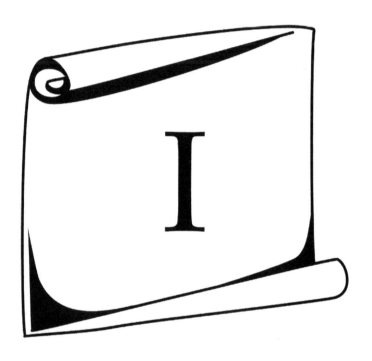

Chapter Nine

I Was Glad When They Said Unto Me

I was glad when they said unto me,
let us go into the house of the Lord
(Psalm 122:1).

I was glad when they said unto me, let us go
into the house of the Lord were not words
I ever uttered as a child.
In fact, this was true for much of my adolescent
years for a good while.
As I reflect on the many times years ago when
I would have to be in church all day, I would
silently let out a groan.
And if I asked, and if you answer honestly,
I probably was not alone.
What I do remember about the church I was
raised in was that, it was more about love,
and less about who to condemn.
Children were hugged and greeted with a kiss,
instead of being ignored as though they didn't exist.

I waited patiently while Mrs. Benson dug in her purse,
only to find a half stick of gum, with lint, dirt and fuzz
on it and probably some stuff that was worst.
And then there was Mrs. Stewart giving me a loving,
but hurtful pinch on the arm. Done playfully, of course,
with no intent to maim or harm.
Both of them and many, many others followed up those
actions with words of love and encouragement,
And you just knew you were in their prayers, these
loving folk, I believe, were angels, heaven sent.
Jesus said, a new command I give to you,
that you love one another. That would include
the littlest sister or young brother.
We should come out of the house of the Lord, anxious
to do good; just like we went into the house of the Lord,
should be understood.
We must unselfishly pray for our youths, the next gener-
ation, and encourage their Christian maturation.
Someone prayed for you and prayed for me for God's
will in our lives to be. Now it is our time to pray for
each other's children, the next generation, abundantly.

Somebody Prayed for Me

Somebody prayed for me, had me on their mind,
They took the time and prayed for me.
I'm so glad they prayed
I'm so glad they prayed for me[11]

Related Rhetorical Questions

- Do you see yourself in any part of this poem?
- Can you think of someone else to whom this poem resonates?
- Is this poem worth reading again?
- Do you agree with the statement: "The more I study the Word of God, the more I know that I need to study the Word of God more".

Personal Notes

_____

_____

_____

_____

_____

_____

_____

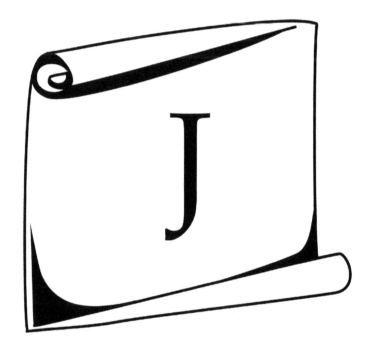

Chapter Ten

Jesus Said unto Her

*Jesus said unto her, I am the resurrection,
and the life (John 11:25a).*

Jesus said to her, I am the resurrection. There is no need
for correction, there can be no objection.
The resurrection and the life. So why do we continu-
ously live with so many burdens and untold strife?
Why do we live in fear when Jesus said
He would be with us, always here.
How quickly sometimes we forget, that as we
look back over our lives, He has never failed us yet.
Some have contemplated suicide, not
remembering with God to confide,
to let Him carry you when you get too weary
to walk by His side.
For God so loved us that He gave His son,
that we might have life abundantly.
What more could He have done?
While the devil is going to and fro trying to see trying
to see whom he can devour, remind yourself that we
worship a mighty God who has all power.

If the devil tries to bring you down, remember that
there are strong Christians all around. Just ask one of
them to pray with you when you're under attack.
Each one is either now experiencing a similar problem,
just came out a problem, or is getting ready to
face one relying on God to have their back.
Don't let Satan trick you into depression and despair.
He has no idea what God has done for us,
nor does he care.
When we feel all alone, sad and it seems that
with life we have lost our connection,
We can take comfort in knowing that Jesus is the life,
and the resurrection.

Just as I am

"Just as I am, without one plea
But that Thy blood was shed for me
And that Thou bid'st me come to Thee
O Lamb of God, I come! I come
Just as I am, though tossed about
With many a conflict, many a doubt
Fighting and fears within without
O Lamb of God, I come, I come"[12]

Related Rhetorical Questions

- Do you see yourself in any part of this poem?
- Can you think of someone else to whom this poem resonates?
- Is this poem worth reading again?
- Do you agree with the statement: "The more I study the Word of God, the more I know that I need to study the Word of God more".

Personal Notes

_____

_____

_____

_____

_____

_____

_____

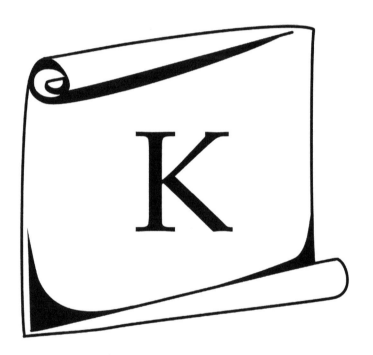

Chapter Eleven

Know ye that the Lord he is God

Know ye that the LORD he is God: it is he that hath made us, and not we ourselves; we are his people, and the sheep of his pasture (Psalm 100:3).

Know ye that the Lord he is God. Don't speculate,
don't contemplate, KNOW!
It is He that hath made us, and not we ourselves,
no matter what those philosophical books say
that are on your bookshelves.
No one can pull themselves up by their bootstraps
without any feet, for it is He who made us,
his people, to be his sheep.
If we thought we made it on our own,
we must have been asleep, because we didn't climb
our mountain alone, it was much too steep.
Boast if we will, brag if we must, but if we take
the credit for what God has done, shame on us.
We need to fall on our knees begging for forgiveness for
our arrogance and pride, and confess our sins that we
have tried so hard to hide.

Oh Lord, Our God, we like sheep have gone astray and so we ask you here today, to take all of our guilt away that we may be wholly thine.

My Faith Looks Up to Thee

My faith looks up to Thee
Thou Lamb of Calvary
Savior divine!
Now hear me while I pray,
Take all my guilt away,
O let me from this day
Be wholly Thine![13]

Related Rhetorical Questions

- Do you see yourself in any part of this poem?
- Can you think of someone else to which this poem resonates?
- Is this poem worth reading again?
- Do you agree with the statement: "The more I study the Word of God, the more I know that I need to study the Word of God more".

Personal Notes

_____

_____

_____

_____

_____

_____

_____

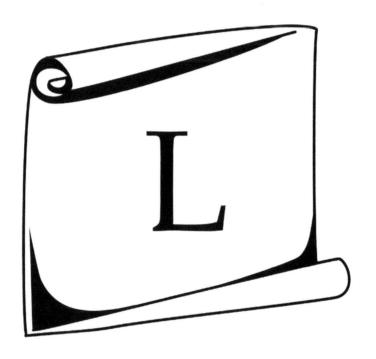

Chapter Twelve

Let Not Your Heart Be Troubled

*Let not your heart be troubled: ye believe in God,
believe also in me (John 14:1).*

Let not your heart be troubled: ye believe in God,
believe also in me, are comforting words that are equal
to my worse troubles *and* their sequel.
For in a disaster, who else would you want to be with
you, other than the Master?
If we can't make it with Jesus by our side, it is truly
going to be a rough ride.
Why do we worry when there seems like such a
long delay, between the time we ask God, bow our
knees and pray?
Has He ever forsaken you? I didn't think so. So, with
an unfailing record like his, "Wither shall I go", is the
way the old saints sang it so long ago.
We can leave our troubles at the altar and not worry
about Satan's attack. Ye believe in God? Gods
got our back.
Let not your heart be troubled when things go amiss,
just listen to the voice of God saying, "I got this"!

The late Bill Withers in a secular way would Say:

Lean on me
When you're not strong
And I'll be your friend
I'll help you carry on...For it won't be long
Till I'm gonna need somebody to lean on[14]

Related Rhetorical Questions

- Do you see yourself in any part of this poem?
- Can you think of someone else to which this poem resonates?
- Is this poem worth reading again?
- Do you agree with the statement: "The more I study the Word of God, the more I know that I need to study the Word of God more".

Personal Notes

_____

_____

_____

_____

_____

_____

_____

Chapter Thirteen

Make A Joyful Noise

Make a joyful noise unto God, all ye lands
(Psalm 66:1).

Make a joyful noise unto the God wherever you are,
at home, at church are while you are in your car.
You may not have the talent of an American idol,
or be able to render an entire recital.
All you need to do, is to think about what God has
already brought you through.
The more you think, the more praise you will acquire,
and before you know it, your heart will be on fire.
You can praise God at home even if in your current
situation you are being harassed.
Because you know if God is for us anyone that is
against us will eventually be embarrassed.
You can make a joyful noise if you join the church choir,
even if you can't carry a note in a bucket,
the director knows exactly what to do.
She will place two good singers on either side of you.
Before you know it, they will drown you out, no matter
how awful your joyful noise is. Even if it is just a shout.

As you are driving down the road and think about how
God has blessed you, it could cause you to be so caught
up in song, that the driver behind you blows his horn,
urging you to move along.
If you are home all alone, just got off of the phone with
a telemarketer who made you groan. You can still make
a joyful noise, rejoice and be glad,
you don't even need a microphone.
Just make a joyful noise.

Jesus Christ is the Way

When I think about
The hour
Then I know
What I must do
When I think about
What God
Has done
For me
Then I will
I will open up
My heart
To every
To everyone I see
And say
Jesus Christ is the way[15]

Related Rhetorical Questions

- Do you see yourself in any part of this poem?
- Can you think of someone else to whom this poem resonates?
- Is this poem worth reading again?
- Do you agree with the statement: "The more I study the Word of God, the more I know that I need to study the Word of God more".

Personal Notes

_____

_____

_____

_____

_____

_____

_____

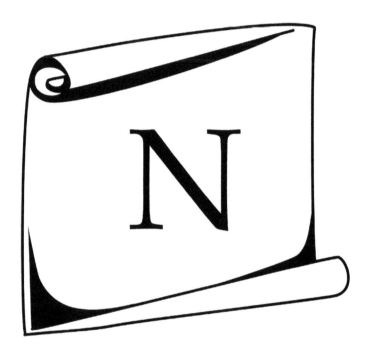

Chapter Fourteen

No Man Can Come After Me

No man can come to me, except the Father which hath sent me draw him: and I will raise him up at the last day (John 6:44).

"No man can come to me, except the father which hath sent me draw him: and I will raise him up at the last day." (John 6:44).
"For God so loved the world, that He gave His only begotten Son, that whosoever believeth in Him shall not perish but shall have eternal life" (John 3:16), is the only way.
It would be a shame for you to have to live the rest of your life under sin's deadly curse, And miss out on having your sins forgiven and spending eternity with God. What could be worse? If you have accepted Jesus as your Lord and Savior, you'll be raised up at the last day, you don't have to worry.
But if you have not, as the those from previous generations would say, "You had better get in a hurry".

Come to Jesus

Come to Jesus, come to Jesus
Come to Jesus just now
Come to Jesus, come to Jesus
Just now[16]

Related Rhetorical Questions

- Do you see yourself in any part of this poem?
- Can you think of someone else to whom this poem resonates?
- Is this poem worth reading again?
- Do you agree with the statement: "The more I study the Word of God, the more I know that I need to study the Word of God more".

Personal Notes

_____

_____

_____

_____

_____

_____

_____

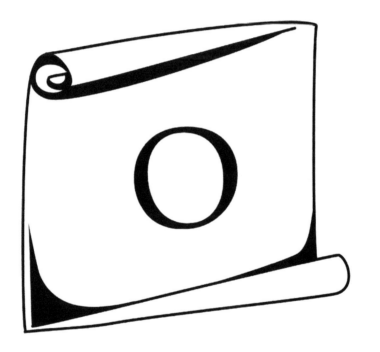

Chapter Fifteen

O Taste and See That the Lord Is Good

O taste and see that the LORD is good: blessed is
the man that trusteth in him (Psalm 34:8).

O taste and see that the Lord is good. Just like 'mama',
'grandmama' and 'big mama' said He would.
All you need is a little taste, any more would be a
shame to waste, After, all how much of His goodness
does it take, for your sleepy soul to wake.
By now you should have recalled something you saw in
the past, that your mind can now recall to re-broadcast.
If God hasn't done anything for you for which you can
thank Him for, hold your breath for a few minutes
and see if you don't fall to the floor.
Don't you realize that every breath you take you didn't
make? Every beat of your heart didn't require
a battery to help it start.
When you were dozing off from too much medication,
went through a traffic light and you were
almost hit by a truck,

Did you thank God and give Him praise, or did you
credit it to your good fortune or good luck?
Isn't it about time that you stop living by the roll of the
dice? And trust in the Lord which was
always your momma's advice.
People our age are dyeing every day who were too
ashamed or too proud to admit to being a sinner.
What an awful thought to be ashamed and denied before
God by Christ, when it was so easy
to have been a winner.
O taste and see that the Lord is good, there are many
that have gone on that wish that they now could.
Whoever we need to talk to, friend, foe or a relative, we
need to do it now. Pray to God that
He would show us how.
This is no time to sit and look pretty, when souls need
saving, in the country, the suburbs and in the city.

*For whosoever shall be ashamed of me and of my
words, of him shall the Son of man be ashamed,
when he shall come in his own glory, and in his
Father's, and of the holy angels (Luke 9:26).*

Related Rhetorical Questions

- Do you see yourself in any part of this poem?
- Can you think of someone else to whom this poem resonates?
- Is this poem worth reading again?
- Do you agree with the statement: "The more I study the Word of God, the more I know that I need to study the Word of God more".

Personal Notes

_____

_____

_____

_____

_____

_____

_____

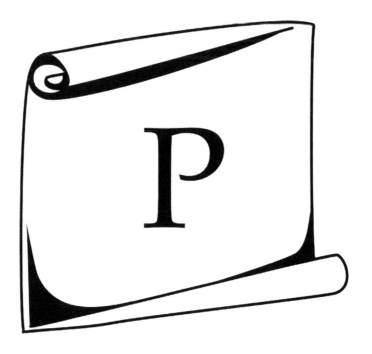

Chapter Sixteen

Pray Without Ceasing

Pray without ceasing (1 Thessalonians 5:17).

Pray without ceasing, what does that mean?
To always pray in public in order to be seen?
No, not exactly. In fact, that might make you
look arrogant and lacking tact.
Jesus said we should not pray to be seen by others, like
we often do when we eat in public with
our sisters and brothers.
By simply praying silently and bowing our head.
We become living witnesses by just breaking bread.
Those observing who have already been saved by grace,
will usually just have a smile on their face.
All other observers, including your servers,
curious to know, become an opportunity,
the way to salvation for you to show.
Whatever we will tell them by way of our story,
may be a blessing to them so that God will get the glory.
But to pray without ceasing shouldn't start at lunch, by
that time of day we should have already prayed a bunch.

For example, before our feet hit the floor in the
morning, we should thank the Lord for another day,
and for the previous night's protection,
For another day of grace to live by His direction;
for another chance to ask for forgiveness
for yesterday's transgression.
Then when I am fully awake, I can pray for my prayer
list names, according to His will to take.
After that I pray, when necessary, even when it's pro-
hibited by law, or, I'm in a hurry and no time to worry.
Besides what kind of god would you pray to who can't
hear a silent prayer. That would be the same
as if he weren't there.
I serve a God who hears me when I don't have a long
time to pray or fuss. Sometimes in a crisis I might only
have time to call out, "Jesus"!
Always praying, is not prayer without ceasing.
It's always not ceasing to pray.

Did You Stop to Pray this Morning

Did you stop to pray this morning
As you started on your way
Did you ask the Lord to guide you
As you started onto your way
Did you think to pray this morning
Did you kneel just one moment to say
Give me comfort for my soul
On this old wicked road
Did you just remember to pray[17]

Related Rhetorical Questions

- Do you see yourself in any part of this poem?
- Can you think of someone else to whom this poem resonates?
- Is this poem worth reading again?
- Do you agree with the statement: "The more I study the Word of God, the more I know that I need to study the Word of God more".

Personal Notes

_____

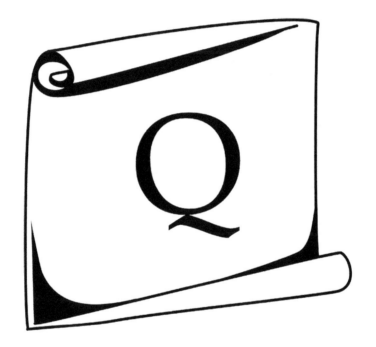

Chapter Seventeen

Quench Not the Spirit

Quench not the Spirit (1 Thessalonians 5:19).

Quench not the Spirit, don't put the fire out. Some
praise inwardly, others would rather let out a shout.
Who am I to judge who is a contender and who is
a pretender, all I want to do is worship Him,
with prayer, praise and a sacred hymn.
When I bow my head to pray, I want to hear what
God has to say. No disrespect to you sitting
next to me on the pew today.
Your constant chatter is interfering with a matter that I
want to bring before God, if you will. A difficult thing
to do when the Spirit you continue to kill.
God is spirit and we who worship must worship
Him in Spirit and in truth. That is something we
have been taught, long ago, since our youth.
So, with no disrespect I would like to reflect on the
preached word today, and I pray that you
will hold whatever it is you have to say.
The sanctuary is filled with the Spirit right now, but if
there is a way to quench the Spirit, we surely know how.

We can quench the Spirit when the choir sings
the same song much too long.
We can quench the Spirit with extra pronouncements
of previous announcements.
We can quench the Spirit when the spoken word with
three main points, is repeated so much, that the Spirit
can no longer reach or touch.
We can quench the Spirit by rolling our eyes,
at someone we are supposed to love,
but somehow, we despise.
We can quench the Spirit by not acknowledging a
friendly smile, to someone sitting right beside
us that we haven't seen for a while.
Quench not the Spirit.

Spirit of the Living God

Spirit of the Living God,
Fall afresh on me,
Spirit of the Living God,
Fall afresh on me.
Break me, melt me, mold me, fill me.
Spirit of the Living God,
Fall afresh on me[18]

Related Rhetorical Questions

- Do you see yourself in any part of this poem?
- Can you think of someone else to whom this poem resonates?
- Is this poem worth reading again?
- Do you agree with the statement: "The more I study the Word of God, the more I know that I need to study the Word of God more".

Personal Notes

_____

_____

_____

_____

_____

_____

_____

Chapter Eighteen

Remember the Sabbath

Remember the sabbath day, to keep it holy
(Exodus 20:8).

Remember the sabbath day, to keep it holy, but
remember, it is not for one denomination solely.
In Christ Jesus there is neither Jew nor Greek,
male nor female, bond nor free. That applies to you
and it applies to me.
We shouldn't keep the sabbath only when it is observed.
Jesus is Lord of the sabbath day and to do good,
the law He disturbed.
On the sabbath we should not be so heaven-bound that
we are no earthly good. Pretending to be better than
others, is not behaving like we should.
If we are honest and admit it, we are all sinners
saved by God's grace, so we have no right to get into
someone else's face, sabbath day or not,
unless of course we forgot.
If we forget, let's quickly ask for forgiveness,
lest we lose our effectiveness as a witness.

Remember the sabbath day to keep it holy,
but walk humbly before our God while
still proclaiming Him boldly.

Take Time to be Holy

Take time to be holy, speak oft with thy Lord;
Abide in Him always, and feed on His Word.
Make friends of God's children,
help those who are weak,
Forgetting in nothing His blessing to seek.[19]

Related Rhetorical Questions

- Do you see yourself in any part of this poem?
- Can you think of someone else to whom this poem resonates?
- Is this poem worth reading again?
- Do you agree with the statement: "The more I study the Word of God, the more I know that I need to study the Word of God more".

Personal Notes

_____

_____

_____

_____

_____

_____

_____

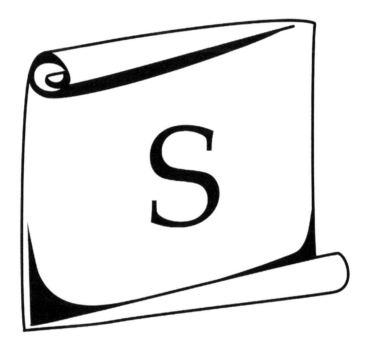

Chapter Nineteen

Sing Unto Him. Song Psalms

Sing unto him, sing psalms unto him, talk ye of all his wondrous works (1 Chronicles 16:9).

Sing unto him, sing psalms unto him,
talk ye of all his wonderous works.
Sing praises to Him for protection from the places
where our enemy lurks.

Sing praises to him for life instead of death.
For hope and yet another breath.
Sing unto him for letting us see the sun shine.
And keeping us in our right mind.

Sing praises unto him for loving us,
enough to sacrifice His only son, Jesus.
We sing praises in everything we do,
and for all of our undeserved blessings too.

For your mercies which are new every day.
And for always making a way.

Praising you in sorrow and in grief, for which it is so
often difficult to find relief.

When we are in trouble or despair, and for your concern
for our every care.
For keeping us from danger unaware and our burdens
you help us to bare.

For all the things we go through in all of life's phases,
to You O Lord, we sing our highest praises.

Praise Him

From the rising of the sun,
Until the going down of the same;
He's worthy, Jesus is worthy,
He's worthy to be praised.[20]

Related Rhetorical Questions

- Do you see yourself in any part of this poem?
- Can you think of someone else to whom this poem resonates?
- Is this poem worth reading again?
- Do you agree with the statement: "The more I study the Word of God, the more I know that I need to study the Word of God more".

Personal Notes

_____

_____

_____

_____

_____

_____

_____

Chapter Twenty

Trust In the Lord with All Thine Heart

Trust in the LORD with all thine heart; and lean not unto thine own understanding (Proverbs 3:5).

Trust in the Lord with all thine heart, is already poetically written for worship in the hymn, 'Tis So Sweet". There is nothing else for me to impart, but join in too and sing. Praise God, "how great Thou art."

'Tis So Sweet"

'Tis so sweet to trust in Jesus,
Just to take Him at His Word;
Just to rest upon His promise,
And to know, "Thus saith the Lord!"
Jesus, Jesus, how I trust Him!
How I've proved Him o'er and o'er;
Jesus, Jesus, precious Jesus!
Oh, for grace to trust Him more!
Oh, how sweet to trust in Jesus,
Just to trust His cleansing blood;
And in simple faith to plunge me

77

'Neath the healing, cleansing flood!
Yes, 'tis sweet to trust in Jesus,
Just from sin and self to cease;
Just from Jesus simply taking
Life and rest, and joy and peace.
I'm so glad I learned to trust Thee,
Precious Jesus, Savior, Friend;
And I know that Thou art with me,
Wilt be with me to the end.[21]

Many shall be the sorrows of the wicked; but he that trusteth in the LORD, mercy shall compass him about (Psalm 32:10).

Related Rhetorical Questions

- Do you see yourself in any part of this poem?
- Can you think of someone else to whom this poem resonates?
- Is this poem worth reading again?
- Do you agree with the statement: "The more I study the Word of God, the more I know that I need to study the Word of God more".

Personal Notes

_____

_____

_____

_____

_____

_____

_____

Chapter Twenty-one

Understand Therefore This Day

Understand therefore this day, that the LORD thy God is he which goeth over before thee (Deuteronomy 9:3a).

Understand therefore this day that it is God
who has made a way.
Each and every day, despite how we think,
or what we say.

Life is not a bed of roses and without God
we couldn't blow our noses.
What could we do without God on our side?
Even with Him we often have too much pride.

Self-made man my foot, we can't 'toot'.
God knows the number of hairs on our heads,
even the ones with a dyed root.

Let's make one thing clear, we had better thank God
for everything we hold dear.
Be glad that God is our refuge and strength and
"therefor will not we fear"

If it Had Not Been for the Lord on My Side

If It Had,Not, Been For The Lord, On My Side
Where Would I Be? Where Would I Be?
If It Had Not Been For The Lord On My Side
Where Would I Be? Where Would I Be?

He Kept My Enemies Away
He Let The Sun Shine Though A Cloudy Day
Oh, He Wrapped Me In The Cradle Of His Arms
When He Knew I' Been Battered and Torn[22]

Related Rhetorical Questions

- Do you see yourself in any part of this poem?
- Can you think of someone else to whom this poem resonates?
- Is this poem worth reading again?
- Do you agree with the statement: "The more I study the Word of God, the more I know that I need to study the Word of God more".

Personal Notes

_____

_____

_____

_____

_____

_____

_____

Chapter Twenty-two

Verily I Say unto You

Verily I say unto you, all these things shall come upon this generation (Mathew 23:36).

Verily I say unto you, all these things shall come upon this generation
but what about this our nation?
The Word of God did not stumble when it used the word humble, before it used pray.
No wonder the nations' prayers fumble, we are so arrogant that we just grumble every day.
Those of us claiming to be followers of Jesus Christ, when reminded of His command to love, turn into scared little mice.
Some of those who are supposed to be evangelizing are too busy hypostatizing and criticizing.
What is to become of this nation's current generation that we thought would be better with so much more education.
Hate must be taught, most would agree. We can see that in children, if we just let them be.

Instead, they are seeing living examples of everything
opposite of love. Watching
each adult push and shove.
All for the sake of trying to look better, totally ignoring
the Apostle Paul's 13th Chapter I Corinthian letter;
'If I speak in the tongues of men or of angels, but
do not have love, I am only a resounding gong or a
clanging cymbal'
In other words, I'm just making noise, like little girls
and boys, trying to cause my enemy to tremble.
I believe that this generation will see some challenging
days, unless we turn from our wicked ways.
Life as we know it could very well be rocked.
Remember, the Word says, be not deceived, God is
not mocked.

Related Rhetorical Questions

- Do you see yourself in any part of this poem?
- Can you think of someone else to whom this poem resonates?
- Is this poem worth reading again?
- Do you agree with the statement: "The more I study the Word of God, the more I know that I need to study the Word of God more".

Personal Notes

_____

_____

_____

_____

_____

_____

_____

Chapter Twenty-three

Wait On the Lord

Wait on the LORD be of good courage, and he shall strengthen thine heart: wait, I say, on the LORD (Psalm 27:14).

Wait on the Lord be of good courage
and he shall strengthen your heart
However, waiting for some is difficult to do,
right from the very start.
We try so hard to believe that faith is the substance of
things hoped for, the evidence of things not seen.
But waiting while hoping and enduring to bring about
patience can often appear to be cruel and even mean.
"We were given this hope when we were saved.
If we already have something, we don't need to
hope for it [You see]
But if we look forward to something we don't yet have,
we must wait patiently and confidently." [23]

My Hope is Built

My hope is built on nothing less
than Jesus' blood and righteousness.
I dare not trust the sweetest frame
but wholly lean on Jesus' name.[24]

Related Rhetorical Questions

- Do you see yourself in any part of this poem?
- Can you think of someone else to whom this poem resonates?
- Is this poem worth reading again?
- Do you agree with the statement: "The more I study the Word of God, the more I know that I need to study the Word of God more".

Personal Notes

_____

_____

_____

_____

_____

_____

_____

Chapter Twenty-four

The Letter X

(X) Examine me, O LORD, and prove me; try my
reins and my heart (Psalm 26:2).

(X) Examine me, O Lord, and prove me,
try my reins and my heart, states the Psalmist
To be honest, I would not be able to pass that test,
even though I would do my very best.
God knows my heart and nothing is hidden from Him,
why waste time by trying to deceive him on a whim?
I know I need to study the Word, even go to church
school. I'm no fool. I need the Word as my tool.
I need to pray for courage to ask a buddy to go with me
to bible study, even if it makes me look
like an old fuddy-duddy.
How can I share the Word of God, if I don't
know the Word of God?
What makes me think I can invite someone to revival
if I'm not familiar with the Holy Bible?
How can I lead anyone to Christ, when I
don't know the way of salvation to give them advice?

When do I say" amen" to the preacher's preaching,
when I have no idea what he or she is teaching?
I have examined my heart in a pre-test, and now I have
to confess, I need a heart cleaning
in order to be of service.
I don't know about you, but I've got some work to do.

Give me a Clean Heart

Give me a clean heart So I may serve Thee
Lord fix my heart So that I may be used by Thee
For I'm not worthy Of all these blessings
Give me a clean heart And I'll follow Thee[25]

Related Rhetorical Questions

- Do you see yourself in any part of this poem?
- Can you think of someone else to whom this poem resonates?
- Is this poem worth reading again?
- Do you agree with the statement: "The more I study the Word of God, the more I know that I need to study the Word of God more".

Personal Notes

_____

_____

_____

_____

_____

_____

_____

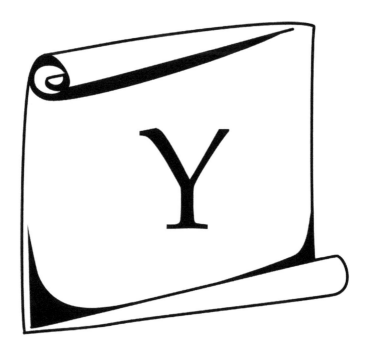

Chapter Twenty-five

Ye Are the Light of the World

Ye are the light of the world. A city that is set on a hill cannot be hid (Matthew 5:14).

Ye are the light of the world. What an awesome
pronouncement and responsibility.
I wonder, if every Christian were just like me,
what kind of world would this world be?
Would they see me forgiving others, as I have been
forgiven. Or, would they see me being hypocritical
as I go about my daily living?
Would they see me loving my sister and brother,
regardless of race, creed, sex or color,
which we are to do by advice.
That, according to the Bible, all will know
that I am truly a disciple of Jesus Christ?
Could they really imagine me as an example of light
for the world to see? Or, would they simply shake their
heads and murmur, "what a waste of electricity".
Would they notice me taking my burdens to the altar
with the intent of "leaving them there".

Or would they see them being dragged back behind me
because I didn't trust my Savior to hear my prayer.
This, "ye are the light of the world" thing is more than a
notion. It requires some serious commitment,
prayer and devotion.
I'm going to have to pray for a little more grace
as I run this race, holding my light up high,
and still maintain my pace.

Lord Hold My Hand

*Oh, Lord hold my hand while I run this race. Oh, Lord
hold my hand while I run this race. Oh, Lord hold my
hand while I run this race, I don't want to run this race
in vain, this race in vain.*[26]

Related Rhetorical Questions

- Do you see yourself in any part of this poem?
- Can you think of someone else to whom this poem resonates?
- Is this poem worth reading again?
- Do you agree with the statement: "The more I study the Word of God, the more I know that I need to study the Word of God more".

Personal Notes

_____

_____

_____

_____

_____

_____

_____

Chapter Twenty-six

Zaccheus Stood

Zaccheus stood, and said unto the Lord: Behold,
Lord, the half of my goods I give to the poor; and if
I have taken anything from any man by false accusation,
I restore him fourfold (Luke 19:8).

Zaccheus stood, and said unto the Lord: Behold,
Lord, the half of my goods I give to the poor;
Most of us today have a difficult time giving our tithes
and offerings, certainly not much more.
Restoring fourfold to any man that he had taken from
by false accusation, did Zaccheus.
He presents a tough act to follow for many of us.
If the cost to get to heaven was paid by leading 10
persons to Christ, via air, train or ocean liner.
In order to pay the transportation cost, sadly,
some of us would still be in need of a co-signer.
Thanking God for loving us enough to send His Son
in perfect sacrifice. We don't have to earn our fare to
heaven, the cost has been paid by Jesus Christ!

Hallelujah! Amen!

Related Rhetorical Questions

- Do you see yourself in any part of this poem?
- Can you think of someone else to which this poem resonates?
- Is this poem worth reading again?
- Do you agree with the statement: "The more I study the Word of God, the more I know that I need to study the Word of God more".

Personal Notes

_____

_____

_____

_____

_____

_____

_____

Endnotes

1   From the devotional editors at Our Daily Bread
    Ministries

2   "My Faith Looks Up to Thee", hymn written by
    Ray Palmer (1808-1887).

3   "Check Out Your Mind". Curtis Mayfield Lyrics
    Warner Chappell Music, Inc.

4   "Have Thine Own Way". Adelaide A. Pollard (1906).

5   "Speak to my Heart". Song by Donnie
    McClurkin, 1996.

6   "I'm Free" Lyrics by Rev. Milton Brunson

7   Mississippi Children's Choir lyrics/
    houseofthelordlyrics.

8   "Lord, Lay Some Soul Upon My Heart", Anon.

9   "On the Battlefield" Authors: Sylvanna Bell;
    Author: E.V. Banks.

10 "Great is Thy Faithfulness", Public Domain. Hymn
    written by Thomas Obadiah Chisholm.

11 "Somebody Prayed for Me" Songwriters: Dorothy
    Norwood / Alvin Darling Kosciusko Music, Ltd,
    Peertunes Ltd, Savgos Music, Inc.

12 "Just as I Am" hymn, written by Charlotte Elliott
    in 1835.

13 "My Faith Looks Up to Thee", hymn written by Ray Palmer (1808-1887).

14 "Lean on Me" Songwriter: Bill Withers lyrics © Songs of Universal Inc.

15 "Jesus Christ is the Way". Walter Hawkins Copyright: Lyrics Original Writer and Publisher.

16 "Come to Jesus" <u>Author: Anonymous.</u>

17 "Did You Stop to Pray this Morning". Songwriters: Ray Westmoreland / Mark Hurley / Sylvester L. Cross a.k.a. Fred Dexter.

18 "Spirit of the Living God". <u>Daniel Iverson</u> (1926) Birdwing Music (ASCAP).

19 "Take Time to be Holy", William D. Longstaff: Public Domain.

20 "Praise Him". Written by Donnie Harper (recorded by New Jersey Mass Choir).

21 "Tis So Sweet to Trust in Jesus" hymn written by <u>Louisa M. R. Stead</u>, 1882 *copyright status is* <u>*Public Domain.*</u>

22 "If it Had Not Been for the Lord on My Side". Times New Roman Lyrics by Helen Baylor.

23 Romans 8:24-25 New Living Translation.

24 "My Hope is Built" Edward Mote (1834).

25 "Give Me a Clean Heart". Margaret j. Douroux, Earl Pleasant Publishing by Charlotte Elliott in 1835.

26 Lord Hold My Hand (African-American Traditional) recorded by The Canton Spirituals.

Final Thought

It is my hope that you were blessed by at least one of the twenty-six poems in this book and that you are now encouraged to continue to study the Word, begin to study the Word, or renew your commitment to begin to study the Word. I also hope that you can now agree with the statement:

"The more I study the Word of God, the more I know that I need to study the Word of God more".

"Work hard so you can present yourself to God and receive his approval. Be a good worker, one who does not need to be ashamed and who correctly explains the word of truth" (2 Timothy 2:15 NLT).

Lightning Source UK Ltd.
Milton Keynes UK
UKHW051949090522
402742UK00013B/301